Whose BABY Is This?

Written and Photographed by
Wayne Lynch

Gareth Stevens Publishing
A WORLD ALMANAC EDUCATION GROUP COMPANY

Please visit our web site at: **www.garethstevens.com**
For a free color catalog describing Gareth Stevens Publishing's
list of high-quality books and multimedia programs, call
1-800-542-2595 (USA) or 1-800-387-3178 (Canada).
Gareth Stevens Publishing's fax: (414) 332-3567.

Library of Congress Cataloging-in-Publication Data

Lynch, Wayne.
     Whose baby is this? / written and photographed by Wayne Lynch.
          p. cm. — (Name that animal!)
     Includes bibliographical references and index.
     Summary: Asks the reader to identify various wild animal babies from descriptions
of their appearances and behavior, and includes a photograph and miscellaneous
facts about each.
     ISBN 0-8368-3638-3 (lib. bdg.)
     1. Animals—Infancy—Juvenile literature. (1. Animals—Infancy. 2. Animals—
Miscellanea.) I. Title.
QL763.L96   2003
591.3'9—dc21   2002036526

This edition first published in 2003 by
Gareth Stevens Publishing
A World Almanac Education Group Company
330 West Olive Street, Suite 100
Milwaukee, Wisconsin 53212 USA

This U.S. edition © 2003 by Gareth Stevens, Inc. Original edition © 2000
by Wayne Lynch. First published in 2000 by Whitecap Books, Vancouver.
Additional end matter © 2003 by Gareth Stevens, Inc.

Gareth Stevens series editor: Dorothy L. Gibbs
Gareth Stevens graphic designer: Katherine A. Goedheer

Printed in the United States of America

1 2 3 4 5 6 7 8 9 07 06 05 04 03

When human babies are first born, they look a lot like their parents, except smaller. Human babies take a long time to grow up, and many of them live with their parents for twenty years or more.

Newborn wild animal babies sometimes look very different from their parents, and many of them grow up and leave their parents before they are one year old.

Can you name the wild animals whose babies are pictured in this book?

I look like I am sleeping, but I am holding onto the fur of my mother's back with all my strength. My mother spends many hours, every day, searching for juicy ants on the ground. She licks up the ants using her long, sticky tongue. Her tongue is as long as your arm.

Who am I?

5

I am a baby giant anteater. I live in the grasslands of South America. I ride on my mother's back all the time until I am almost one year old. My mother wraps her bushy tail around me at night, like a blanket, to keep me warm.

Giant anteaters do not have any teeth, even when they grow up. Their strong front claws help them fight off attacks by hungry jaguars.

I hatched in a nest made of sticks. The nest is high in a tree. I have a fluffy coat of soft feathers to keep me warm. In this picture, my sister and I are only two weeks old, but I already use my sharp, hooked beak to eat meat. My parents bring it to the nest. My neck looks puffed up because I just finished lunch.

Who am I?

I am a baby hawk. I live in the prairie areas of central North America. I can fly when I am only two months old, but I am not very good at it. I have sharp claws, called talons, on my toes. I use my talons to protect myself and to kill prey.

When hawks first start to hunt, they catch grasshoppers and crickets to eat. With a little practice, they learn to catch ground squirrels and mice.

I was as tiny as a bee when I was born. I could fit in a teaspoon — along with twenty of my brothers and sisters! As soon as we were born, we crawled through our mother's fur and climbed into the warm pouch on her belly. After two months, the pouch was too crowded, so we all rode on her back.

Who am I?

13

I am a baby opossum. I live in the forests of North America. During the day, I sleep in trees. I can wrap my tail around a branch and use it like an extra foot to help me climb. At night, I hunt for food. I eat frogs, earthworms, small snakes, grasshoppers, bird's eggs, and even garbage.

An opossum's bare ears and tail are not made for cold weather, so they freeze, sometimes, in winter.

ntil I am two months old, I stay hidden in the bushes. I wait there every day for my mother to come home from hunting. Then she feeds me her milk. When I grow up, I will hunt, too. I will hunt hares and small gazelles because I will have long legs that will help me run as fast as a car on the highway.

Who am I?

I am a baby cheetah. I live on the plains of Africa. I am the fastest animal on Earth, but I am not as strong or fierce as other big cats. Lions and hyenas often steal my meals, and even noisy vultures can frighten me away. I have a funny voice, too. Instead of roaring, I chirp like a bird.

Even though cheetahs can run very fast, slower animals often escape from them by twisting and turning.

At one month old, I still can only crawl. I look helpless lying on the ground with my eyes stuck shut. Until I was a few weeks old, my mother kept me hidden in an underground burrow with the other babies in our family. Owls, weasels, foxes, eagles, and many other animals would like to eat me for dinner.

Who am I?

I am a baby arctic ground squirrel. I live in the far north. My eyes are near the top of my head so I can watch for danger. Seeds, leaves, and berries are some of my favorite foods. I eat beetles, too, when I can catch them.

Arctic ground squirrels are real sleepyheads. They spend more than half of the year curled up in their burrows, hibernating.

When I was hatching, I used the small white tooth on the tip of my beak to crack open my eggshell. The next day, I left my family's nest beside the water to swim in the lake with my parents. When I get tired of swimming, they let me ride on their backs. They also dive underwater to catch fish, leeches, and insects to feed me.

Who am I?

I am a baby loon. I live in the northern lakes of North America. I am a large waterbird. My heavy bones and big webbed feet help me dive deeper than other waterbirds. But, for a big bird, I have small wings, so I must run across the water to gain speed before I can fly.

At night, a loon's cries will echo across the water, making a lake seem haunted. Loons have many different calls. Some of the calls sound scary, like screaming ghosts.

My mother's pouch is dark and hot inside, so I often pop my head out to look around. A baby like me, either a boy or a girl, is called a joey. But some people call me a "pouch potato" because I live in a pouch for almost nine months. For nine more months after that, I still stick my head into the pouch when I want milk.

Who am I?

I am a baby kangaroo — "roo" for short. I live in the deserts and grasslands of Australia. I like to eat grass, grass, and more grass!

As I hop along on my big feet, my big tail helps me keep my balance. When I stop to rest, I often lean back on my tail and use it as a stool.

Aborigines, who are Australia's native people, were the first people to see me. They gave me the name "kangaroo."

Index

More Books to Read

Animals and Their Young (series).
  Elizabeth Dana Jaffe
  (Compass Point Books)

Growing Up Wild (series).
  Sandra Markle (Atheneum)

Life Cycles (series). David M.
  Schwartz (Gareth Stevens)

*Young Animals and Their Parents.
  Animals Up Close* (series).
  Renne (Gareth Stevens)